Let's Learn About Jesus

Get to Know God's Perfect Son

ZONDERKIDZ

The Beginner's Bible Let's Learn About Jesus

Copyright © 2024 by Zonderkidz

Published in Grand Rapids, Michigan, by Zonderkidz. Zonderkidz is a registered trademark of The Zondervan Corporation, L.L.C., a wholly owned subsidiary of HarperCollins Christian Publishing, Inc.

Requests for information should be addressed to customercare@harpercollins.com.

ISBN 978-0-310-36713-0 (softcover)
ISBN 978-0-310-36717-8 (ebook)

Art direction: Diane Mielke
Illustrations by: Denis Alonso

Printed in Malaysia

24 25 26 27 28 / COS / 5 4 3 2 1

A Note to Parents

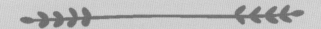

Who is Jesus? Why is it so important for us to know as much as we can about him?

The Beginner's Bible Let's Learn About Jesus was written to help young children begin to understand who Jesus is and just how important he is to our salvation—and to the story of how much God loves us and has always loved his people.

To make this subject more approachable, this book is divided into small, easy-to-follow sections:

Introduction to Jesus, pgs. 4–21

Characteristics of Jesus, pgs. 22–43

Our Relationship with Jesus, pgs. 44–48

Using *The Beginner's Bible* as a companion, readers will learn about Jesus's character and think about how we can be more like him. Each of the featured characteristics includes:

- An example from *The Beginner's Bible*
- Guided questions for discussion
- Prayer prompts to help readers connect with Jesus

We hope this book provides a meaningful introduction to Jesus. We also pray it inspires children to develop a relationship with him—to see that if they follow his examples of how to live and how to love, their lives will be continually enriched by God's gifts of grace and salvation.

Who is Jesus?

Have you ever heard of Jesus?

Maybe you heard his name in church, at home, or even in school. Or maybe while listening to a song or talking to your friends!

Jesus is someone very special.
It's important to know him!
Let's learn about Jesus together!

From the Beginning

Adam and Eve were the first people God created. God loved them very much. Adam and Eve loved God too!

God made a beautiful garden for them to live in. He gave Adam and Eve everything they needed. But he also gave them one rule. He said, "Do not eat the fruit from the tree of the knowledge of good and evil."

It didn't seem like a hard rule to follow. But one day, a sneaky snake visited Eve in the garden. He said, "You should eat some of this tasty fruit. If you eat it, you will be like God."

So Eve took a bite. She gave some to Adam too.

Of course, God knew Adam and Eve had done something they were told not to do.

They broke God's one rule, and God was sad. Adam and Eve were sad too. They had to leave the garden.

But God still loved them so much! He already had a plan to make things right again.

JESUS was part of his plan.

When it was time, Jesus would come to earth. He would teach people how important it is to follow God and love one another. And if we follow Jesus and live like he wants us to, we will be just right with God!

Just Wait

But when would Jesus come?

Adam and Eve had children. Their children had children too. People started filling up the world, and God loved them all.

There was a special group of people called the Israelites. They believed in God and loved him, and even though they messed up sometimes, God never broke his promise to take good care of them. When they were hungry or thirsty, scared or lost, or happy and filled with joy—God was always there.

But sometimes God's people forgot about how much he loved them. They forgot to love God back. They forgot to obey his commandments.

God sent some very special friends called prophets to talk to his people. A prophet is a person who takes God's messages and delivers them to his people.

Stories about some of those prophets are in the Old Testament of the Bible.

These prophets told God's people all about his love. Sometimes the people listened. Sometimes they did not.

One prophet named Isaiah worked really hard to let people know God had a good plan to help them. Isaiah had a super special message—he told the people God would be sending a savior to the world.

This Savior would be very special … a messiah come to earth, and he would be the Prince of Peace. He would save us from our sins by dying on the cross so we could be with God forever.

That Savior is Jesus!

It's Time

Just when God's people were feeling like God didn't love them, and nothing was going right in the world … something special happened.

An angel named Gabriel visited a young woman. She lived in Nazareth. Her name was Mary.

Gabriel told her, "Don't be afraid. You are very special to God. You will become pregnant and give birth to a son. You must name him Jesus. He will be called the Son of the Most High God."

Would Mary be brave? Yes! Mary looked at Gabriel and said, "I love God. I will do what he has chosen me to do."

It was time … Jesus was finally coming to earth.

Jesus Arrives

Mary loved Joseph. Joseph loved Mary. Soon after they were married, they had to go on a trip to Joseph's homeland. So Joseph and Mary traveled to a little town called Bethlehem.

Bethlehem was crowded. Mary and Joseph looked for a safe place to sleep, but all the inns were full. A nice innkeeper let Mary and Joseph stay in his stable.

While they were there, Mary gave birth to the little boy the angel Gabriel told her about. God's Son Jesus was born!

God sent angels to tell the people that Jesus had arrived! The angels told the shepherds, "Today, in the town of Bethlehem, a Savior has been born!"

The shepherds rushed to see Jesus for themselves. They were so happy, they shouted for joy! They told everyone they met about Jesus.

And there were even three wise men who traveled many, many miles to see Jesus. They followed a very special star God put in the sky. When they found Jesus, they worshiped him and gave him precious gifts fit for a king.

Jesus Grows Up

Jesus was God's Son, but he was also a human being, like us. And just like all children, Jesus grew up and learned things like we do.

Once, when Jesus was about twelve, his family went to Jerusalem to celebrate Passover. Jesus went to the temple and spoke to the teachers there. He stayed with the temple leaders and talked all day about God the Father. They were amazed at how much Jesus understood.

But his mother and father found him and took him back home with them. Jesus still had things to learn!

God's Perfect Son

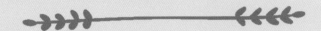

Matthew 3:1-17; 4:18-22; 9:9; 10:1-4

Jesus came to earth just like you and me. But he came as an extra special person—God's **perfect** and **obedient** Son.

When Jesus was about thirty years old, he knew it was time to start working on God's plan. The plan to make everything good again in the world.

Jesus asked his cousin, John the Baptist, to baptize him in the Jordan River. After Jesus was baptized, the Holy Spirit came down from heaven in the form of a dove. God said, "This is my Son, and I love him. I am very pleased with him."

Because Jesus didn't sin, he showed people what God's perfect love was like. He and his disciples worked hard together, teaching people about God's love and care so the world would be saved.

Think About Jesus

- What is one thing Jesus did to show he was the perfect Son of God?
- How can we show our love to God?
- How are you an obedient son or daughter for your parents? As a child of God?

Praise Jesus

Jesus, you are the perfect Son. Help me to be more like you every day!

A Very Wise Teacher

Matthew 5:1–12; 6:25–34; Luke 11:1–4

Jesus was **wise**. He knew and taught so much about God to the people.

People from all over wanted to hear Jesus teach about God's love. They came to listen to his special words. One day, Jesus was preaching on a hill by the Sea of Galilee.

Jesus had a lot to teach that day!

"Stop worrying!" he said to the people. "You are much more important than the birds and flowers God cares for. So do not worry. God takes care of them. God will take care of you!"

That same day, Jesus taught his disciples and the people a very special prayer. That prayer is called the Lord's Prayer. This prayer is still said today!

Our Father in heaven,
hallowed be your name,
your kingdom come, your will be done
on earth as it is in heaven.
Give us today our daily bread.
Forgive us our debts,
as we also have forgiven our debtors.
And lead us not into temptation,
but deliver us from the evil one.
Amen.

Think About Jesus

- Where do you think Jesus learned so much about his Father?
- Do you have a teacher who has taught you a lot? What makes that person a good teacher?
- Think about a time you showed wisdom when you made a decision.

Praise Jesus

Jesus, teach me to love God as much as you love him. Teach me to love other people like you do too!

A Loving Miracle Worker

Mark 6:30-44; Luke 9:10-17

Jesus was kind and **loving**. He performed **miracles** to help others.

One day, over 5,000 people came to see Jesus. All day, they listened to him talk about God's love. The disciples said, "It is late. These people should go home and eat dinner." Jesus replied, "We can feed them." The disciples found a boy who had five loaves of bread and two fish. Jesus took the food and gave thanks to God.

The disciples gave bread and fish to every person in the crowd! And to their surprise, there were still twelve baskets of food left over!

Think About Jesus

- Do you think miracles still happen today?
- Talk about a miracle you know about.
- How do you think the little boy felt when he shared his lunch with Jesus and 5,000 people?

Praise Jesus

Jesus, I believe in miracles, and I believe in you.

A Trustworthy Man

Matthew 14:22-33; John 6:15-20

No one is more **trustworthy** than Jesus!

After all the people went home, Jesus went to a mountaintop to pray. He sent the disciples ahead, on their boat. As they were sailing away, a big storm came. They were in danger!

Jesus walked right out onto the water toward his friends. They shouted, "It's a ghost!" "No," Jesus said. "It is I. Don't be afraid." Peter said, "If you really are Jesus, let me walk out to you." "Come," said Jesus.

Peter walked out onto the water toward Jesus, but he became afraid of the wind and the waves. He started to sink! Jesus reached out and took Peter's hand. "Why didn't you keep trusting me?"

The two men got into the boat together, and the storm stopped. "Truly you are the Son of God!" the disciples praised. And everyone was safe.

Think About Jesus

- Why do you think Peter started to sink?
- What does the word "trust" mean?
- How can you show you are a trustworthy person for your friends?
- You can trust Jesus because he loves you. Who else can you trust? Why?

Praise Jesus

Jesus, I trust you to help me when I am weak or scared. Thank you for holding my hand and helping me.

A Merciful and Forgiving Man

Luke 19:1-10

One of Jesus's jobs on earth was to show us how to be **merciful** and **forgive** others. Jesus believed that we should forgive one another. He knew that was a way to show God's love to others.

One time, lots of people came to hear Jesus teach. One of them was Zacchaeus. He was a tax collector who often treated others poorly. He took extra money for himself! Most people in town didn't like him very much.

Zacchaeus wanted to see Jesus, but he was too short to see above the crowd. So he climbed up a tree. Jesus looked up and called, "Zacchaeus, let's go to your house."

People didn't understand why good Jesus wanted to spend time with sinful Zacchaeus. Jesus told Zacchaeus how much God loved him. He forgave Zacchaeus for treating people poorly. And Jesus's forgiveness changed Zacchaeus's heart!

Zacchaeus told Jesus, "I will give money to the poor. And I will pay back everyone I cheated." Jesus was so happy!

Think About Jesus

- Why did Jesus show forgiveness and mercy to Zacchaeus?
- What does it mean to forgive someone?
- Have you ever forgiven someone for hurting you? How did you feel afterward?

Praise Jesus

I ask for forgiveness, for all the things I have done that hurt you, Lord. Please forgive me.

A Caring Friend

John 11:1-44

There is no one more **caring** and **thoughtful** than Jesus!

Jesus had many friends. One day, he got a message from his friends Mary and Martha. "Our brother Lazarus is very sick. Please come."

Two days later, Jesus arrived. Martha was crying. "Lazarus has died. If you had been here, you could have healed him."

Jesus was sad. He cried with his friends. He didn't want them to feel hurt. Then something wonderful happened. He prayed, "Father, I know you always hear me. Show everyone you have sent me."

And a miracle happened! Jesus called, "Lazarus! Come out!" And his friend walked out of the tomb. Lazarus was alive, and everyone was filled with joy.

Think About Jesus

- How do you think Lazarus felt when he walked out of the tomb?
- What can you do to show others that you're friends with Jesus?
- How can you show others you are a thoughtful and caring friend?

Praise Jesus

Thank you for being my friend, Jesus.
For supporting me and loving me
no matter what.

Jesus Loves Us

Matthew 9:18-26; Luke 8:40-56

Jesus was very **loving**.

Jesus's whole life was spent teaching about love with words and actions. One day, he showed the world how to love.

A man named Jairus came running up to Jesus. "Please! Come heal my daughter. She is dying," he cried. So Jesus and his disciples went with Jairus.

While he was walking, Jesus felt someone touch his tunic. "Who touched me?" It was a woman who had been sick for a long time. She said, "It was me, Jesus."

And Jesus smiled at her. He said, "Your faith has made you well. Go in peace."

Then Jesus kept walking with Jairus and the disciples.

When they arrived at Jairus's home, all the people said it was too late. "The girl has already died."

Jesus said to Jairus, "Trust me. Your daughter is just sleeping." Then he went into the house.

Jairus and his wife went in with Jesus. Jesus knelt down next to the girl and said, "Wake up, child."

Her eyes opened and she climbed out of bed! She was well!

Think About Jesus

- Jairus and the sick woman had very strong faith in Jesus. Do you have strong faith in him too?
- How do you think Jairus felt when he heard that his daughter had died? Do you think he was angry with Jesus?
- Showing love to other people is important. How can you show you love your mom or dad?

Praise Jesus

Jesus, thank you for your healing love and goodness. Help me to have faith in you.

Our Savior

Matthew 28:1-10; Luke 22-23; John 20:1-18

God sent Jesus here as the **Savior** of the world.

Jesus knew he was on earth to do an important job for God. His job was to teach about God's love. He was going to rescue us from sin by sacrificing himself. He would guide us back to God.

Some people didn't like what Jesus was doing. They didn't want to hear about God anymore. And so they decided to stop Jesus.

These people arrested Jesus. They took Jesus to their leaders. The leaders said, "You are not the Son of God. We do not believe anything you say."

And they told the soldiers to take charge of Jesus.

The soldiers made him carry a heavy wooden cross. They nailed him to the cross. And Jesus died.

All of Jesus's friends were sad. But nothing could stop God and his plan. Jesus said they would see him again. And they did!

Three days after he died, Jesus rose from the dead! It was all part of God's wonderful plan to save us from sin. Nothing could stop God from loving people, and nothing could stop Jesus either.

Jesus saw his friends again. He told them, "I gave my life so you can be with me in heaven—so that all people can be with me there!"

Then Jesus said, "Get busy! Show others how to live. Keep teaching about God's love!"

And when the time was right, Jesus returned to heaven. He went up in a cloud. Angels told the disciples, "Don't worry. Jesus will return the same way you saw him go!"

And his followers went to
Jerusalem to pray
and wait.

Think About Jesus

- What was Jesus's job on earth?
- Why did some people not love and believe in Jesus?
- What do you think it would be like to listen to Jesus actually preach today, in your church?
- Think about how much Jesus loves you. How can you thank him for this incredible love?

Praise Jesus

Jesus, I believe in you! Thank you for saving me from my sins! I will help you spread the good news of God's love to my friends and family.

43

Listen to the Spirit

Right before Jesus went up to heaven, Jesus promised the disciples the Holy Spirit would come. The Holy Spirit would guide them. He would show them how to be like Jesus. How to be kind, loving, wise, caring, and forgiving.

The Holy Spirit gave the disciples strength, courage, and knowledge. They worked hard to spread the Good News of Jesus to the whole world.

As Jesus's followers, we are still doing that job today. The Holy Spirit is in us! When we listen to the Holy Spirit, we can be kind and loving toward others. And we can show them how to follow God.

Follow His Word

We can read in the Bible about the many lessons Jesus taught. One important lesson is called the Great Commandment.

One day, when Jesus was asked what the most important commandment was, he said, "'Love the Lord your God with all your heart and with all your soul. Love him with all your mind.' This is the first and most important commandment. And the second is like it. 'Love your neighbor as you love yourself.'"

Another good lesson from Jesus is called the Golden Rule. Jesus told his followers, "In everything, do to others what you would want them to do to you."

When we follow Jesus's commandments, we show others how much God loves his people.

Be Like Jesus

We should be like Jesus in all that we do. In the way we live, the way we treat people, and even how we treat ourselves.

Jesus shows us just how much God loves us and why we should love him. He teaches us how to love others and treat them with kindness. But just knowing about Jesus and reading the Bible isn't enough. We really need to follow his example, and then we also need to get to know him and God in a special, personal way.

Talking to God is a very important way to build a relationship with God. While Jesus was on earth, he loved talking to his Father—God. That is called prayer, and Jesus prayed very often.

He prayed with his friends every day. And Jesus liked to go to quiet places so he could pray all alone.

So find a quiet place and pray. Or sit with someone and pray in a group. Go to church and pray and sing loud! You can talk to God and Jesus any place, any time.

God loves to hear from you! Jesus loves to hear from you too. And every time you pray, you become more like Jesus.